*It is hoped that the postcards contained in this book
will revive memories of times gone by,
and to younger people perhaps show a glimpse
of a more leisurely way of life.*

Lynette A. Archer
September 2000

ISBN 1 870947 70 3

First published 2001. Copyright I W County Press Ltd

Published by Isle of Wight County Press Ltd
123 Pyle Street, Newport, Isle of Wight PO30 1ST

Produced by Crossprint Design & Print
Daish Way, Dodnor Estate, Newport, Isle of Wight PO30 5XB

A Short History of Newport

Newport is the capital of the Isle of Wight, a shopping centre and a market town.

Richard de Redvers called it **"new port"** for his castle at Carisbrooke, so it has always been known as such since the first Charter was granted in 1180. In March 1926 a Roman villa was discovered during building works in Cypress Road, indicative of a very early Roman occupation in AD50, which continued to be occupied for another 250 years.

It was James I who granted Newport Borough status and the first Mayor was appointed in 1607.

Two members of Parliament were elected and from 1584 to 1885 then it became part of the Isle of Wight Constituency. Among notable members have been the Duke of Wellington and Lord Palmerston.

Not much of Newport's early history has been recorded but its days were often hazardous.

1349 *An outbreak of plague was rampant.*

1377 *The town was wholly destroyed by the French. The town was slow to revive.*

1559 *A commission was set up under Sir Francis Knolleys to remedy matters.*

1583-4 *A plague did little to help.*

Slowly Newport began to grow and by the 17th century it was quite a lively market town, the only crowded built-up area in the Island up to Victorian times.

The prosperity continued and in the 18th century when the military were stationed on the Island, Newport became quite the social centre with assemblies and even a duel or two. It became the centre for the Island's country gentlemen; their gaily-coloured clothes contrasted with the rougher attire of the country people, who with their wagons and produce thronged Newport streets.

In the 19th century there were 3,000 inhabitants, and the town was of pleasing appearance.

There was a broad market square, the Beastmarket (now St James's Square), and the Cornmarket (now St Thomas's Square). At the north-east corner of this square stood the Cheese Cross where on market days the farmers' daughters would display their wares and on the north side of the square were the butchers' stalls known as The Shambles. The Butter Market was at the junction of High Street, Quay Street and Watchbell Lane.

The main streets were the High Street and Pyle Street and the streets constructed at right angles to the above. These are still with us today - Mill Street, St James's Street, Holyrood Street and Town Lane. Two other streets were provided parallel to High Street, these being Lugley Street and Crocker Street, and from this basic pattern Newport continued to develop.

The mouth of the River Medina provided a good deal of commercial traffic right to the centre of the town. This was conveyed along the river to Cowes or to the mainland, making Newport a very busy centre with many warehouses along the quay.

Industrially it has progressed and many agricultural concerns are equally flourishing. Now Newport is the centre of excellence.

NEWPORT, I.W.
THE RIVER AND TOWN.

The Quay showing the river and town. The house was called The Ark.

Horsey & Son series. Postmarked Newport, September 22nd 1905.

Newport Streets and Place Names

From *The Enchanted Isle* by C.W.R. Winter
reproduced by kind permission of the author

Broadlands   Messrs Nunn & Co's blond lace factory. The firm started business in about 1811. In 1826 it manufactured lace at Broadlands of "French blond", an expensive and very fine lace.

Castlehold   Land between the west part of the High Street and Pyle Street, once the demesne of the castle.

Cockram's Yard   An alleyway connecting St Thomas's Square to South Street. Possibly named after a Boyce Cockram who lived in Newport c1850.

Coppin's Bridge   Well known to all who travel in Newport, its name commemorating a William Copping who lived in 1577.

Cosham Street   One-time name for South Street and for many years the southern boundary of the town.

Crocker Street   Named after a John Crocker AD 1341.

House of Industry   Established in 1770, the second Incorporated Workhouse in England.

Lugley Street   A 13th century name, possibly from the same root as "luck" meaning a pool or dam. Alternatively there was a William Lugley who was Provost or Reeve in Newport at the end of the 13th century.

Nodehill   Or "Noddies Hill", noddies being dead men and, specifically, the Frenchmen ambushed in 1377 who were buried hereabouts.

Pyle   From "Pil", a pile or stake but also believed to mean a ford.

Scarrot's Lane   Named after Christopher Scarrot who had a house and orchard in the street in 1720.

Snook's Hill   Prior to 1828 a Mr Snook was a well-known blacksmith with a forge at the top of the hill (lefthand side, going up).

Trafalgar Road   Name given in 1861 to Deadman's Lane, formerly (in 1461) "Dedmanstret", either from the ambushing of a party of Frenchmen in the 1377 raid or (more likely) from a dead body having been found there.

A composite card of Newport in the Jay Em Jay series.

By Jackson & Son (Gy) Ltd Grimsby & Bradford.

The Upper High Street showing Frank Weeks, a clockmaker and jewellers shop; Hayward, photographer who also issued postcards; and a tobacconists. The tall house, further down on the left, is Victoria House. The Castle Inn with sash windows is situated on the corner of Mill Street. Note the billboards on the side of the Castle Inn. Horse traffic had passed by as evidence shows in the road.

The date of this scene is 1918 to 1920.

The Victoria Memorial, designed by Percy Stone and unveiled by Princess Beatrice on August 13th 1903. The inscription reads "To Victoria the Queen this memorial was raised by the people of the Wight". Looking south on the left we see the County Club; Jordan and Stanley, wholesale and family grocers; Wadhams, furniture and carpets; the Red Lion; and Roach's hotel and restaurant. Facing the square with the bow window on the corner of Pyle Street were the offices of the County Press. There were railings on the righthand side to tie up the beasts for market.

Both cards by L. Levy.

29 NEWPORT (Isle of Wight).
High Street — LL   SELECTA

The High Street looking east. No worry with traffic problems! A little boy pushes a cart and ladies stroll across - note the pram. On this sunny day the awnings are out on the left, where you can see Gentle's boot and shoe shop and C. Webb, tailor. On the right, Alderslades, plumbers and decorators, and lower down the World Stores. The turret of Edward Morris, soft furnishers, can be seen on the skyline. The Town Hall completes the picture.

The Beast Market, held on Tuesdays and Saturdays. This shows a busy scene. Looking south, there are sheep in pens and cows tied to the railings outside J.H. Linington, general furnishing, agricultural ironmonger and gunmaker, heating of churches, schools, greenhouses, etc, by hot water. They also sold a selection of stoves, ranges, tile hearths, etc. The beast market was finally moved to a purpose-built site in South Street in 1928. Later the square was used as a bus station.

The market day 1907. Looking north on a busy day. Roach's hotel and restaurant on the right (a la carte from 12 till 3pm, afternoon teas a speciality). The proprietor was George Quarrier. Looking straight across the square we see the corner of the Bugle Hotel, and a booking agent for the railways. Note the doorway of the Red Lion and the lamp bracket.

The Town Hall was designed by John Nash and built in 1814. In 1887 the clock tower was added to commemorate Queen Victoria's Golden Jubilee, thus throwing out the proportions of the building. The butter market was held on this spot. The town fire engine was also kept through the middle arch in the early 1920s. The horses were kept in a stable in Holyrood Street. They were harnessed to the one and only fire engine! Note the sign to the Southern Railway. To the left of the Town Hall lies Quay Street. The High Street continues to the right.

The Post Office remains the same today. Two dogs walk along and children pose for the camera. The house on the right was a doctor's residence. Next to the Post Office is H. Greengrass, bookseller, stationer and newsagent, and sole agent for Goss's Heraldic Porcelain. In later years they moved to Nodehill, but have long since gone.

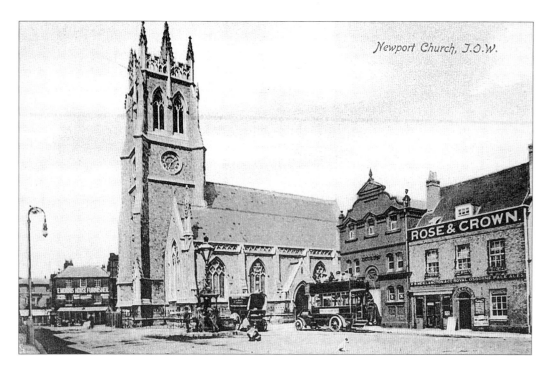

St Thomas of Canterbury and St Thomas à Becket Parish Church, erected in 1854-6, stands in St Thomas's Square. It is built on the site of the old church which dated from Henry II. The tower stands at 132 feet and is a landmark around the town. Edward Morris, furnisher, can be seen. The fountain is from St James's Square and was moved when the Victoria Memorial was erected. The carriers' carts always congregated outside Gould, Hibberd and Randall's building, and the bus is seen leaving the square.

The Rose and Crown. DL 78. Originally known as The Crown, from the Middle Ages. Later the rose was added as a damask rose was presented to King Charles I when he rode through Newport on November 23rd 1647 by Frances Trattle. The inn ceased to trade in 1996 and has reopened as a French theme bar.

The card is postmarked Newport 1906.

11

St Thomas Church. Princess Beatrice with the Bishop of Portsmouth leaving the church after the dedication of the banner of the British Legion (IW Branch). Her Royal Highness is seen walking towards the Newport War Memorial preceded by Captain Adams Comor who is carrying the wreath which was placed at the foot of the memorial.

The date is September 28th 1929.

The War Memorial. Made of Portland stone, erected in 1919, then bearing 341 names.
The unveiling ceremony was performed by H.R.H. Princess Beatrice. The United Choirs and the Royal Ulster Rifles Band conducted by Mr William Allan, bandmaster, are leading the singing of the hymns. Recently all who lost their lives in World War II have now had their names engraved on the memorial.

ST. PAUL'S CHURCH NEWPORT. ISLE OF WIGHT. P.167.

In 1844 St Paul's, Barton (a daughter church of
Whippingham) was erected to the north of the village in
Staplers Road. The old village is situated to the east of the
Medina near Coppins Bridge, and was formerly known as
"Barton's Village". It was not connected with Barton,
near Osborne, but derives its name from a speculating
builder who developed the land in the early 1800s.

Several noteworthy people are buried in the churchyard -
John Milne, "the father of modern seismology", H.W.Nunn,
lace manufacturer of Broadlands House,
and Mr Benjamin Mew of 'Polars' in Staplers Road.

The church was designed by the architect C.W.Wild.

Isle of Wight County Technical Institute and Free Library. Opened on Saturday, January 30th, 1904. The north wing, on the left of the building, was opened in 1907. The board school, the building with the turret, had been in existence for many years.

The lamp on the corner of South Mall (now St John's Road) is being serviced by a man on a long ladder, watched by a group of children.

Looking down the road you can see Node Hill with St John's Church wall on the left.

The free library was founded by the Seely family.

St Johns Road. Formerly the main road to Shide Cross. The mall was known as South Mall.
The terrace of seven houses was called Albion Terrace. The house beyond on the left called Forest
Villa was the home of Mr Albert Midlane, the author of the hynm "There's a Friend for Little
Children". The pavement on the right is unmade. The horse is eating from his nosebag. The men
pose with a long ladder, for what purpose we do not know. The postcard dates from 1897.

A later view looking towards Nodehill and Medina Avenue Junction. Note the metal posts on the
mall and the pavement made up on the left of the card in approx 1930s.

(Sunshine Series. A. E. Sweet Man & Sons, Tunbridge Wells. Mint).

Portland House Academy.

This school was run by R. Barnes & Son. It was situated at the junction of West Street and Trafalgar Road. In an old advertisement of 1903 it is described thus:- "in this old established school, every facility is afforded for qualifying boys for commercial or professional life. Preparation for the public schools. The civil service and the medical, legal and pharmaceutical prelims and other exams.

Classes are formed for youths and young ladies requiring lessons in book-keeping, French, shorthand, drawing, etc".

This photograph was taken on May 23rd 1929 by Miss R. Reed and produced as a postcard.

The school closed down on December 15th 1929.

There is a tablet on the wall of W. H. Morey to mark the presence of the school site.

W. J. Rugg & Co shop in Holyrood Street. Wholesale and retail tobacconists. Vectis cigar stores.

Specialities:- Prince George of Wales 18/- per 100. High class cigarettes – Prince Alfred Alexander of Edinburgh 6/- per 100. A perfect blend of choicest tobacco, guaranteed absolutely pure, price one shilling and a penny halfpenny for 2ozs.

Their noted "Carisbrooke Smoking Mixture", very mild four pence per ounce, or one shilling and three pence per quarter pound.

This card was posted at Newport 2.45pm on December 7th 1904.

Advertisement for the County Press. 1923 was the date of the first Newport Carnival.

In Pyle Street outside the rear entrance of the County Press, now known as Brannon House.

Date and publisher unknown.

Newport Post Office Staff. 1914-1918 era. Women delivered the mail during the First World War. Postage rose from a halfpenny to one penny in 1918. Deliveries were made up to six times a day.

Publisher unknown.

Person unknown.

Photographer Fred Quinton, 96 High Street.

The Grandstand in Nine Acres Field. (Nov 17th 1905 is the postmark).
The Butchers' and Publicans' Fancy Dress.

The President (Mr A. H. Dockrill) and team of The Newport Cricket Club.

Taken 1922-23 on the Victoria Recreation Ground.

Caws and Company, Lugley Street. Wholesale, British and foreign fruit and flower importers.
The premises lately used by Fred Trim. The man holding bananas is behind the entrance
to Chain Lane.

Lorry registration either C or GR1267. 8 men and the driver, another lorry inside.

Photographer Fred Quinton, 96 High Street.

J. Cheverton, Trafalgar Road Dairy. Milk was ladled out in half a pint, one pint and quarts into the
housewife's milk jug.

A very rural card. Date unknown.

46 High Street. Postmark December 23rd 1907.
It was sent as a Christmas card.

The same premises updated! Photograph September
3rd 1925.Alderslade's have now ceased trading.

WARBURTON'S HOTEL, NEWPORT.

Warburton's Hotel, Quay Street. By Royal Appointment to the late Queen Victoria.

W. T. James was the proprietor in the early 1900s of this first class family and commercial hotel with 40 rooms. (en pension terms, boats meet all trains. Electric light throughout. Telephone 26).

Postcard sent from Cowes, July 1907.

The postcard was very useful for messages – "Trust you got back safely travelling today" is written on the card.

Warburtons has been renamed Calverts Hotel.

Isle of Wight Parliamentary Election 1906.

Photograph Kime, Lower St James's St, Newport.
Card mint.

**Mr Godfrey Baring, M.P. for the Isle of Wight.
(afterwards knighted).**

Canning Days Corner. South Street. Mr Arthur Blow of Mornhill Farm, with horse and cart. The Mission Hall (St Thomas's Church Hall) in the background. The bell was incorporated in the New Parish Centre in Town Lane. The site is now Safeways.

"ESSEX" BOARD FOR CEILINGS & WALLS

Photograph showing the "ESSEX" Board on the ceiling of the show-room of Messrs. Wm. Dibben & Sons, Ltd Church Litten, Newport, I. O. W.

An advertisement for Messrs. W. M. Dibben & Sons Ltd in Church Litten. This site is also occupied by Safeways, as is the back entrance to the market, situated further along Church Litten.

A 1st World War tank travelling along the High Street.

The tank in Quay Street outside the Methodist Church.

It was in the Victoria Recreation Ground for years. Later it was broken up for scrap in 1940, to help the 2nd World War effort.

Newport Station. The Isle of Wight started operations in 1862 with a 4four and a half mile line between Cowes and Newport. By 1900 the system increased to a maximum of 58 miles. During 1923 the five separate railway companies on the Island were amalgamated into Southern Railway.

The card shows the Cowes train.

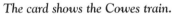

Probably a works outing! The indicators show the Sandown/Ventnor on the left, and the Ryde train on the right.

The entire Newport Railway network disappeared in 1966 as a result of the "Beeching Axe". A by-pass road was constructed. No signs are left of it now.

Taking down the old bridge.

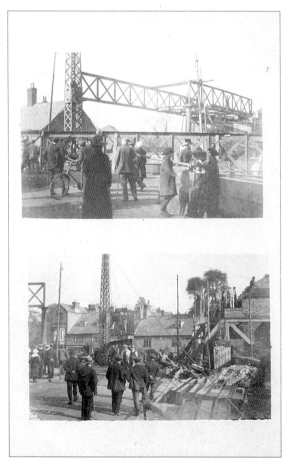

The last piece of the old bridge.

The new bridge at Coppins, March 1919.

The first girder being brought into position across the road for lifting.

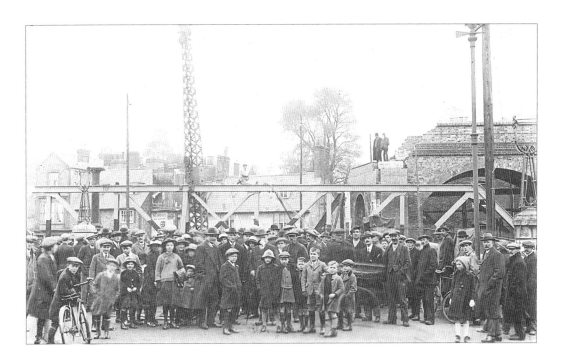

Crowds waiting. The White Lion pub is in the centre background. The new bridge was necessary, as possible defects in the old bridge had been observed and heavier locomotives would be used in the future.

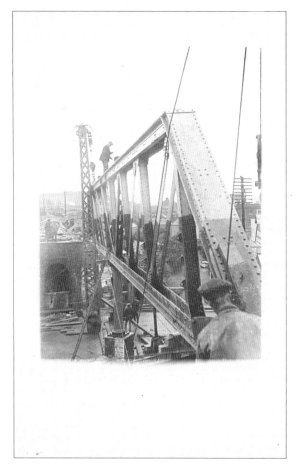

The first span in position.

A girder being lifted into position.

The second girder across the road ready for lifting.

The new bridge at Coppins.

The girders in position.

Completed.

The bridge was dismantled in 1960, four years after the line had closed.

Coppins Bridge

View looking towards Snook's Hill.

The new bridge span, with equipment and onlookers!
The White Lion is on the left of the card. Spring 1919.

The famous arches, running into the station.

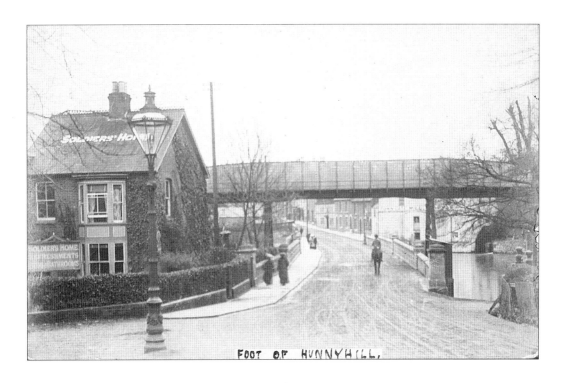

The bridge carrying the line to Yarmouth and Freshwater.

Post-marked 1906.

The Town Quay, showing the railway bridge. The portion on the extreme left was a swing bridge, to allow shipping through. The scene indicates the business. A horse and cart await loading. Alex Sharp & Co Ltd, timberstore, on the right.

Demolished in 1973-74.

(Postmark March 30th 1907 on a Mentor & Co card).

The Quay viewed from Little London. Five boats unloading. Crouchers (at 6 Quay St) and Shepards Bros brought their cargoes daily to the quay from Southampton and Portsmouth. M. S. Whip, M. S. Tall-Ho, M.S. Harkay, M.S. Brush, M.S. Vixen, M.S. Hound, M.S. Huntsman, M.S. Chamois, M.S. XXXX were some of the most frequent vessels to visit the quay.

Entrance to Albany Barracks. This card was posted on May 10th 1908. Ideal series.
Albany Barracks were constructed in 1798 and originally known as Parkhurst Barracks.
The name was changed as a compliment to the Duke of York and Albany (the brother of George IV)
who was the commander in chief.

The Colonel's House, The Barracks.

Posted on August 28th 1915. No.22 L.Levy.

Dr. Groves of Marl Hill, Carisbrooke.   Mint

The funeral procession in Fairlee Road of Dr. Groves. He died in May 1907 aged 67 years. For 25 years he was a medical officer of health for the rural district. President of the I.W. Horticultural Association and kindred organisations, he also supported Island athletics and cycling.

Postmark May 29th 1907.

The West End of the town, showing Carisbrooke Road and the Mall.
Wrays, grocers are on the right.

Mint.

Mr Fred A. Riley's West End Toilet Salons in 1935. Now demolished. Advertising permanent
waving and barbers. Next door was Stagg's Wool Shop, on the corner of Drill Hall Road.

Printed and Published by J. Howard Burgess, 53 Pyle Street, Newport, I.W.

From the County Press:-

1907 Mr Leonard Jordan was presented with an illuminated address, in recognition of his services as Lion Secretary of the I.W. Liberal Union for many years.

In 1913. The only woman candidate who had contested a county council election, Mrs Russell Cooke, failed at Newport in March "largely because of Liberal abstentations at a time when the women's suffrage movement seems to have had a serious set back". She was defeated by Mr T. Hobbs, by a majority of 26.

Printed and published by J. Howard Burgess, 53 Pyle Street (Newport).

The Agricultural Show at Nine Acres Field. Arthur Wood's banner, advertising machinery, etc.
Note the steam engine used for harvesting. (Published by James Cooke and posted Sept 24th 1908).

General view of Newport, from the Whitepit Lane area. Nine Acres field is to the left on card
(by L. Levy. Mint).

The houses are in Elm Grove. St Thomas's Church Tower and the river Medina can be seen.

Messrs Jordan and Stanley's Fire, April 12th 1908. From the County Press:- "One of the most destructive and alarming fires, ever known in Newport occurred on Sunday at the familiar premises in Upper St James's Street of Messrs Jordan and Stanley, the wholesale and retail grocers.

The shop and store, filled with new stock for the Easter trade, was completely gutted and at one point the fire threatened to spread to adjoining buildings. Fire officers and spectators narrowly escaped injury when the roof and side wall collapsed into the road. The Shanklin Steam Fire engine Service was summoned to help fight the blaze, which was not extinguished until late in the evening."

Footnote: Jordan and Stanleys was demolished, a second time when it received a direct hit by enemy action 2nd World War, April 1943.

The postcard above was published the day after the eventful fire. Thus a postcard is sometimes the only illustration of a disaster.

Mr Alan, a reporter for the
County Press, starting out in Fairlee Road
on December 11th 1917.

Card mint. No publisher named.

When Arthur Gregory (antique dealer) ceased trading, the County Press moved to the premises
opposite the Town Hall in 1912. Vacant land at the rear of the premises was obtained,
and Mr J. C. Millgate, architect, designed a building suitable for the printing works.
It was erected by Messers W. H. Brading of East Cowes.

Postcard sent on Sept 24th 1910.

Old Grammar School, Newport.   7545 The "Wyndham" Series

The Old Grammar School was erected in 1619 on the corner of Lugley Street and
Lower St James's Street. The Star Hotel was destroyed by fire in 1910.

(Card Mint. The Wyndham series).

Charles I. holding a Meeting of Commissioners at the Grammar School, Newport, I.W.

Charles I holding a meeting of Commissioners which resulted in the abortive treaty of Newport.
The King's bedroom looked into Lower St James's Street and the old school-room was used as the
presence chamber. The parliamentary commissioners lodged at the Bugle Hotel, the conference
taking place in the Old Town Hall.

(Postcard Mint. Issued by W. H. Upward, High Street).